Financially Unchained

The Complete Guide to the Proven FIRE System (Financial Independence Retire Early) for Financial Freedom

Dear Reader

By leaving a review after reading my book you are helping the book tremendously. If you have the time to do so, I would be forever grateful. Thank you!

Introduction

Congratulations on buying *Financially Unchained!*

This book is not only a powerful resource for you, but it is also a powerful milestone for you to celebrate! You purchasing this book means that right here, right now, you are ready to create financial abundance for yourself. Learning how to take important action toward living a life that is financially free is a powerful position to be in.

These days, financial freedom is a hot topic because many people realize that a lack of financial freedom can cause major issues in people's lives. Those who lack financial freedom find themselves stressed, in ill health, passionless, and frustrated by the way things are going. These individuals are more likely to stay in less-than-desirable situations like bad relationships or living with unwanted roommates because they are incapable of doing anything else for themselves. People no longer want to live their lives strapped with debt, financial burdens, and cash-flow problems. Instead, they want to begin living a life that is free, purposeful, passion-filled, and joyful. They want to enjoy their lives, connect with the people around them, and get back to the process of *actually living.*

The best way for you to view this process is to recognize that not only are you stepping into financial freedom, but you are also giving yourself the *skill* to do so. This means that your financial freedom is not going to be created by some magical potion that lands on your doorstep and suddenly turns you into a financially free individual. Instead, it means that you are going to be the one creating your financial freedom—so no matter what happens to you, you will always have the skills to *continue* creating financial freedom in your life.

For many, achieving financial freedom and realizing that they have the skills to maintain and sustain their financial freedom are two entirely different things. When you have financial freedom come to you in a way that feels like it was caused by luck or some freak of nature, you can develop incredibly unstable feelings around your finances. As a result, even if you are financially free, you may continue to feel the burden of finances fall on your shoulders, as you fear that there is never enough or that you will not be able to keep it. Through this book, you will learn all about how you can actually create financial freedom for yourself and accept that financial freedom with confidence so that you can truly experience feelings of freedom. That way, you are able to enjoy your freedom genuinely.

It is crucial that you follow this blueprint in the exact path that it has been laid out for you to ensure that you are building your knowledge in a way that walks you through the process. Attempting to jump ahead or create your freedom in a way other than what is laid out for you can result in you sabotaging your financial freedom by taking actions in the wrong order. Alternatively, you may begin to ignore the information in this book as you feel that you "already know" what is within these pages. Be sure to stay open, follow this path, and complete every single exercise if you want to achieve true financial freedom.

In this book, you are going to discover the FIRE concept, which stands for "Financial Independence, Retiring Early." This concept is a rapidly growing movement that millennials are taking to as a way to overcome the tough economy and finally afford to do life on their times, which is why it is the perfect time for you to get started! FIRE allows individuals to understand not only what it is that they are working toward (financial freedom and retirement,) but also how they can get there. We are going to explore how you can begin applying this concept to your life so that you can release yourself from the stress of cash flow problems and financial burdens and start living your best life.

It is important that as you read this book, you understand that your present reality with money does not have to be your forever reality with money. You *can* change your entire financial story through perseverance and commitment—as you will learn about in this book. Many people make the mistake of believing that they are incapable of changing their financial outlook because that is how they have always been. The reality is that *anyone* can set the scene for financial success for themselves, and they can come out significantly better than ever before. Just look at Carl Jensen who experienced what he calls "the awakening" around 2012. Originally, he was a software engineer in a Denver suburb, working a high-pressure job and making about $110,000 per year with benefits. Despite it being a good job overall, Jensen was under high stress constantly and was constantly throwing up and ill due to the stress, so he could not even enjoy his wages and benefits. After finding the FIRE method, Jensen saved the majority of the family's income until they had a net worth of $1.2 million, and retired from the company he had worked with for over 15 years when he was 43.

If you are ready to begin paving your path to financial freedom in your personal life, *now* is the time to begin! Please take your time, follow this book at your own pace, and stay focused on your goals. Trust that as long as you continue to take the action steps, you will find yourself enjoying financial freedom in no time!

The Financially Unchained Formula

The road ahead may seem long and winding. As you are reading this you may feel that many complexities lay ahead. But let me break down the basic formula for how to gain control of your financial life.

The basic formula looks like this:

Assets - Expenses - Debt = *Time to retirement*

Simple right? Do not get bogged down on all the financial terms and complexities of asset management. Just look at this formula and remember that you can achieve freedom if you are willing to work on your assets, expenses, and debts. Many of your peers live lifes full of unneeded expenses and towering amounts of debt. Do not do this. You will start changing these bad habits as the first thing after reading this book. Focusing on gaining assets is the next step in your path. Today there are many simple yet powerful investment options. One of the underlying and most used asset management systems are index funds which you will get introduced to later. Everything in this formula will be unpacked into greater detail, so you will know how to take action.

Now this book is not full of fluffy material. It gets you the tools to succeed. When you get overwhelmed just remember this simple formula and remind yourself that YOU are in control.

Chapter 1: Get Out of Debt

The very first step in achieving financial freedom is getting yourself out of debt. Acquiring and holding debt is expensive as debt comes with exorbitant fees required to allow you to be able to leverage that debt in the first place. While not all debt is bad debt, staying in debt too long or without a plan—or getting debt into for the wrong reasons—can lead to a great deal of trouble for you. Many individuals are deep in debt of all types and find themselves having a hard time eliminating their debt because other things always seem to need financial attention. Moreover, many individuals are painfully unaware of the many ways that they are wasting their money on other things when they could be paying back their expensive debts.

Before you begin planning for how you will save money or what you will invest your money in, you need to begin by making a plan to get out of debt. Getting out of debt can seem daunting, but once you get started, you will discover that it is actually a lot easier than you may have believed it would be. Furthermore, once you are out of debt, you are in a much stronger place financially—meaning that you can really begin stepping toward complete financial freedom. For many people, being debt-free feels like a massive step into financial freedom—so trust that by getting your debt in order, you will first be creating a strong foundation for you to leap from.

Unlock Your Inner Warrior

You need to decide right now what type of income you want to be saving and where you want to be in the future. The best way to do that is to set your goals and then find the FIRE path that actually serves you in achieving those goals.

When you set your goals, you need to set SMART goals or goals that are:

- Specific – you have a clearly outlined goal
- Measurable – a clear way of measuring when you have reached it
- Attainable – you know that you can reach it, but it should not be too easy
- Relevant – it makes sense to what you want to have
- Timely – it has a clear deadline

Sit down right now with a piece of paper and hash out what it is that you want: do you want to retire by age 35 with $1.5 million in the bank? Do you want to have the ability to launch your own company and work on your terms by age 41 with $2 million in the bank? Maybe you want a minimalist lifestyle by age 38 and enough to get the bills paid? Get clear, set deadlines, keep these goals focused, and write them down somewhere that you can see them every single day so that you can stay motivated to keep going.

Why is it so important to have goals? Us humans are by nature adapted to procrastinate until our hormonal responses take over. At this moment we gain laser sharp focus and an unbreakable drive to reach our goal. In nature these goals where closely linked to survival such as getting food, shelter or fighting off invaders. In today's lives, we are not closely linked to the gains of purposeful actions. Often, we work to reach a goal that will gain us some value far ahead in the future instead of the instant gratification that our ancient forefathers experienced. Use the SMART goals to hack your biology and create an iron will to reach your goal. Setting goals can unlock the same mental responses that create an immediate drive to attain something. It will sustain you over time when you experience ups and downs.

Once you have decided what your goals are, you need to pick the FIRE method that is going to get you there fastest. At this point, there is no sense dillydallying around and waiting for life to happen: now that you have a goal, you need to get on board with a strategy that is going to make that goal happen.

Steady Paced FIRE Saving
If you are pleased with where you are at, you can always stay where you are at and begin saving from your regular 9-to-5 income. You can do more in the way of savings to ensure that you are not spending nearly as much, and then save every extra dollar that you have. This way is often considered slower because you will receive fewer pay increases and bonuses, although it can be a solid way of getting to where you want to go if you are ready to start right now. For those who are not interested in jumping around from workplace to workplace, this is also a more desirable idea.

Fast Paced FIRE Saving

If you are not ready to sit around and wait for life to happen, you can take it into your own hands by making yourself a far more valuable employee and then increasing the competition around you. People who work this way will often kiss the bosses butt the entire time they work somewhere and then apply for competitive jobs that will offer hefty salary increases to take the employee over. In lucky scenarios, this can equal a wage battle that earns the FIRE saver far more money, thus meaning they have even more to save toward their goals.

Your Own Path

If you are not the type to work for someone else and you want to take matters into your own hands, working for yourself can be a great opportunity to achieve your SMART FIRE goal faster. If you are quick-witted, have a strong understanding of how to become an entrepreneur, and are willing to put in the effort to make it work, this is often the fastest way to get ahead. Because there is no cap on how much you can make as an entrepreneur, you can get there far faster this way. That being said, if you are not willing to do the work or you feel that you would be ineffective at it, avoid this method as it will only make you frustrated and slow you down because entrepreneurship is not for everyone.

Creating A Meaningful Goal

As you set goals for yourself and your future, it is important that you do so with the intention of setting goals that are meaningful to you. Setting goals that do not genuinely have meaning or purpose for you is going to result in you not feeling particularly drawn to actually pursuing your goals because they simply lack enough reason behind them. Your goals should be ones that are highly personal and able to drive you to want to continue pursuing financial freedom in your life.

When it comes to creating your meaningful goals, think about things that are going to have meaning for you for a long time. Many people get caught up in the practice of consumerism and find themselves purchasing things that bring them happiness at the moment but no longer bring them happiness after a few days. We often say "when the novelty has worn off," meaning that after the feeling of having something new has gone away, we no longer cherish that item. You have likely experienced this before with impulse purchases, such as new clothes, random accessories or household items, or even food items. Often, humans want to purchase something new because the feeling of having something new is fun and exciting—until it isn't any longer. Stepping out of this consumerism cycle of being happy and then uninterested in the things that you are buying is a great way to step away from purposeless practices and into meaningful ones. With this in mind, consider creating goals for yourself that involve experiences, or purchases that are actually going to fulfill you and keep you happy long-term. For example, when you are purchasing clothes do not purchase something because it is on sale or because "it will do." Instead, purchase something because you love it, you will get great use out of it, and you can see yourself wearing it on a regular basis. In other words, make the process of purchasing things an experience so that you no longer go through the constant ups and downs of consumerism behaviors.

Science says that when it comes to creating experiences and memories, we are more likely to remember the things that made us feel something intensely over the things that we felt neutral about or things where the feeling quickly ran out. For example, if you were to purchase a new necklace for yourself impulsively or without much consideration, you would likely not care about that new necklace in a few days. If anything, you may actually begin to feel guilty around purchasing that new necklace because you could have used the money for something else. If instead, you turned the process into an experience, you could easily change the entire reality of purchasing the necklace. For example, if you were to consider what style you wanted, spent some time shopping around for the exact necklace, found one that you absolutely fell in love with, and then brought it home and learned how to work it into your wardrobe effectively, you would likely love that necklace. That feeling that came with wanting something, finding the perfect item, and then incorporating it into your life would become a fond memory that would be more likely to lead to you receiving joy from that necklace for a long time.

As you are setting goals for yourself, seek to set goals that are based around the feelings that you want to have, and the specific experiences that you think would support you in creating those feelings. This is how you are going to be able to create a meaningful goal that actually supports you in staying motivated and continue working toward what you want in life.

Defining What Happiness Is for You

Often, the number one goal that people are working toward in life is to be happy. For years, it was believed that happiness was something that could be bought or created, but as the age of consumerism matures, we have come to realize that true happiness is not a commodity. You cannot purchase, sell, or trade happiness. Happiness is something that you must create for yourself, which means that in order for you to create happiness for yourself, you first need to identify what happiness even means to you.

As you explore the meaning of happiness in your eyes, it might help you to consider what other people define happiness by, too. Sometimes, hearing about other people's definitions for things like happiness can help increase your awareness around what true happiness is and how you can define happiness for yourself so that you are pursuing a true form of happiness, as opposed to something that you believe to be happiness. Below are some great examples of happiness definitions made by people who were close to dying, which puts them in a position of having a deeper understanding of and perspective around such things. Pay attention to what they focus on, what they seem to care about most, and how you may be able to use this awareness to help you create a clear and meaningful definition for yourself to use.

The Hierarchy of needs

One of the most used models for defining and outlining the basic needs that create happiness is named after the psychologist Maslow. In his hierarchy of needs he outlines the basic necessities and levels that make up various levels of motivation and drivers of happiness:

The pyramid of needs naturally has the basic drivers in the bottom. These include the basic functioning of the body. Hereafter what we humans strive after is our basic safety and integrity of our body. As you can see when we go further in the pyramid none of these drivers are called material wealth, Mercedes Benz etc. After careful research it has become consensus that material wealth are more of a lower level basis for building other things on top of. When you read about Elon Musks latest project it should be obvious to you that he is not driven by the need for more money. He and many other who have all the other basic needs fulfilled are driven by the need for creating something new or living life the way they dream of doing it.

Consider these levels and the motivational drivers for happiness when you live your life or plan your future. Chances are that you are hardwired like the rest of us.

Live life on your terms

The first common theme amongst people who are dying is their realization that in the end, their own opinions were the ones that mattered most. In life, we often base our happiness and decisions off of what other people think of us, which can lead to us feeling obligated to behave in a certain way. We tend to believe that we will feel happy if people think more of us, or if we look good to certain people that we admire, and oftentimes we will make decisions in life based on what these people think and feel. This may make us feel a small sense of fulfillment or pride at the moment, but oftentimes, the intense effort and what may be lost in the process of trying to please others is not worth the small prize we receive—if we receive any at all. When it comes to creating freedom, realize that both your finances and your emotions will be freed up by you releasing your need to impress others and allowing yourself to make decisions for you, first. When you do this, you stop purchasing things or doing things that are meant to make other people like you more and instead you do the things that will make *you* like you more.

Work less and spend time with loved ones

Another big thing that people wish on their death bed is that they would not have worked so hard. As humans, we are lead to believe that we will find happiness in hard work as hard work can lead to fulfillment and satisfaction. Both of these can also lead to a great sense of pride, especially if we feel that we have worked hard and done a good job at what we were working toward. While working and being satisfied are important, it is not ideal to base your happiness off of your work ethic. Most people on their death bed wish that they would have spent less time working and more time enjoying life with their loved ones or engaging in the things that they enjoyed so that they would have more memories beyond work. This means that not only should you release "working hard" from your definition of happiness, but also that you should consider adding variety or seeking fulfillment in all areas of your life instead of just one. From a financial perspective, doing this also releases your mind from attachments to finances and instead allows you to see that many things in life have nothing to do with money whatsoever.

Based on these two experiences that people who are near passing have experienced, we can conclude that defining happiness for most people looks like existing in a state of authentic expression, honoring your experience, expressing yourself, connecting with others, and allowing yourself to feel. By incorporating these five elements into your own definition of happiness in whatever way feels right for you, you can begin to understand and experience true happiness in a more meaningful way.

Dream freely

An easy way to find what brings you joy and to begin incorporating happiness into your life is to sit down with a piece of paper and a pen and brainstorm everything that you would do if money, time, and resources were not an issue. Where would you be, who would you be with, what would you be doing, and how would you be spending your time? Allow yourself to fully release from the beliefs that anything is off-limits based on logical reasons such as a lack of resources or time and instead just dream freely. When you dream freely in this way, you give yourself a quick and easy access point into discovering what brings you true joy in life. These are the things that you should include in the meaningful goals that you are working toward as you create financial freedom for yourself.

Pay Off Your Debt With the Snowball Method

The snowball method is one of the fastest ways to pay off your debt, as it allows you to accumulate speed and momentum with your debt repayment plan. There are six steps in paying off debt fast using the snowball method, which has been outlined below.

- **Step 1:** Start by gathering up all of your debt except for your mortgage. Go through your papers and find every single debt that you have under you right now and put it all in front of you. It may be scary to look at this tall stack of papers if you have a lot of debt, but trust that this is an important first step in getting to where you want to go.
- **Step 2:** List off your debts in order from smallest debt to the highest debt. You want to

have them in perfect order so that you can see exactly where all of your smaller and larger debts are. Keep this list handy near your finances as this list is your game plan.

- **Step 3:** Continue making the minimum payments on all of your debts to ensure that you are not going backward. Do not pay anything above minimum payments on any of your debts, except for the ones outlined in Step 5. You want to make sure that you have plenty of money left over for this.

- **Step 4:** Find ways to make extra money in any way that you can. You can do odd jobs, save extra money, sell things that you are not using, or even take on a smaller side job until your debt has been completely repaid. Find what works for you, and add to your finances in as many ways as you can.

- **Step 5:** Begin putting all of that extra cash toward your smallest debt first. The goal is to pay this debt off as fast as you can, so start putting all of your extra money onto it and paying it down. Keep paying the minimum payments on your other debts, and put all of the extra into this debt, as this one will be paid off faster than the others.

- **Step 6:** Once your smallest debt has been paid off, take all of the money that you have been putting onto that debt and put it onto your next smallest debt. Now, you will be adding all of that extra money plus your minimum payment from your smallest debt on top of your minimum payment for your second smallest debt, meaning that you will be paying a lot off at once.

Let's look at an example:

1. $500 medical bill – 12 % interest
2. $3.000 credit card debt – 15 % interest
3. $6.000 car loan – 8 % interest
4. $11.000 student loan – 4.5 % interest

In this example, we pay off the medical bill first as it is the smallest amount. To pay off the medical we didn't just pay the minimum amount, but what we were able to. Let's say $500. We then take the amount we were paying on that loan and put it towards the credit card debt as well as the minimum amount we were already paying on it. Notice that we do not consider the income we were using to pay the medical bill freed to spend on other things. No, this is the snowball method, so we keep aggressively pouring the available income into the next debt as well as adding the minimum payments together as we keep going.

Continue this six step process through until you have paid off all of your debts and found yourself debt-free, aside from your mortgage if you have one. Once you have made it debt free, it is very important that you do not go right back into debt, so be wiser with your spending habits from here on out!

Why will this method work? Will it not be cheaper to pay off the debt with the highest interest first? Well, looking at it from a behavioural perspective the snowball method is much more likely of getting you debt free. This is because the reward of paying off a debt will give you immense satisfaction and the will to keep on going!

Negotiate with debt collectors

If you have some debts where you have just an inkling of an idea that you can get them reduced, you should try! It may seem scary to call a debt collector to negotiate an agreement. Debt collectors are not scary people, but someone simply minding their job. Often one of their main tasks is to get some payments collected which means they are very willing to negotiate your debt.

Below you will find some steps on how to better make sure you get the best deal from a debt collector. Start calling the companies where you have the smallest debt as you will get better at negotiating when you have tried it a few times.

1. Be aware of debt collectors who try to push fees on you. Often, they are only mandated to collect state sanctioned fees but will try to push something extra.
2. Explain your situation in a way that conveys that you have multiple debts but are serious about making a payment plan. Help them help you. If they understand you are working toward a goal, they will be more likely to lower your debt as this opens up a win-win scenario.
3. Try to lower the interest rate, the amount due or both. You have multiple buttons to push. If you can't succeed in one thing try to squeeze in

a reduction in your interest rate. Anything can help.

4. Debt collectors love big one-time payments rather than smaller payments over time. If you are in a situation where you can pay a lump sum, try to negotiate a hefty reduction. When negotiating DO NOT reveal how many funds you have available. Try to low ball it.

5. Be friendly but grow a tough skin. Debt collectors are experts at sensing the type of person that easily backs down from a tough conversation or doesn't negotiate well. Always keep your cool and stay friendly (even flirtatious if you can). Be ready to counteroffer when they make an offer. Your goal is to pay less than what you are able to.

6. Get everything in writing before you start paying anything.

If you follow these steps, you should absolutely not be surprised if you will be able to shave a couple of thousands of your debt.

Enjoying the book?

By leaving a review you are helping the author tremendously. If you have the time to do so, I would be forever grateful. Thank you!

Chapter 2: Save Your Cash

Once you have paid off your debt, the next part of the process in developing financial freedom is saving your cash. Achieving a point where you have no debt is great, but if you have no savings as well, you are still not living in a state of financial freedom. At this point, saving your cash becomes a lot easier because you are no longer paying back debt, so you have more funds that you can set aside to support yourself with. You will also likely have a greater sense of respect for your money, as your debt is now repaid, and you realize how much effort it took to pay back your debts in the first place—hence, you do not want to put yourself back in that position.

Saving your cash can be done in many ways—from cutting back on expenses to increase the amount that you budget to set aside in a savings account. Oftentimes, the best way to really dig into savings is to consider the goals that you made in the previous chapter and to keep those in mind every time you invest in your savings. Doing this can help remind you why you are creating financial freedom in the first place, which can make it easier for you to begin putting more money into your savings account.

Cutting Expenses

The first thing you want to do when you are saving money is to look for ways to save as much money as possible. A big mistake that people often make when they are finally free of debt is believing that they have more money now, which leads to them living beyond their means once again. Instead of falling into that unwanted cycle, consider revisiting your budget once all of your debt has been repaid and looking for ways that you can save even more money. Start by allotting the money that you were using for debt repayment toward savings, as you have already learned about how you can shoulder your monthly bills without this money available to you. If you want to, you can slightly increase your expenses to include funds for more leisurely activities now, but ensure that you continue to remain modest about this so that you are not overspending.

A great way for you to start cutting expenses is to look at where you are spending money that does not need to be spent so that you can begin cutting those expenses and to spend more wisely instead. Here are some great examples of ways that you can begin saving:

- Stop buying more food than your family can reasonably eat, and start buying off-brand food items that are just as good.
- Shop with a list so that you are not purchasing things that you do not need, as oftentimes without a list we will buy far more than we actually require, which can be wasteful.
- Plan your meals ahead of time so that you know exactly what to buy; also if you plan meals around the same key ingredients you can buy in bulk and save more money.
- Carry snacks with you; eating out is expensive and if you are hungry and on-the-go it can be

easy to justify buying fast food when, in reality, that expense can add up quickly.

- Use everything until it is gone, stop throwing things away when you still have some of it left as this is wasteful and results in you needing to buy more.
- Challenge yourself to save as much as you can with every purchase you make by learning how to shop around for a good deal.
- Do not be afraid to ask for better deals; most companies like your phone company, internet company, and other service providers are often willing to offer you a better deal if you just ask so go ahead and make the call!

Beyond cleaning up your budget and your expenses on things that are needed, you can also begin focusing on cutting expenses in other ways, too. For example, if you have useless things in your life that are costing you money or that are taking up space, you can consider eliminating them. If you have any subscription services that you are not using frequently, or you have any random bills that are not serving you, eliminate these so that you are no longer spending money on things that are not valuable to you. If you have valuable items sitting around the house that are not bringing you joy and are not being used, consider selling them so that you have more money to set aside in your savings account. The more you eliminate unwanted or unnecessary expenses and belongings, the more you can allot toward your savings account and invest in your financial freedom.

The other side of the coin is looking at what you are actually doing with your time. Many people see joyful experiences as needing to be expensive or cost money—when in reality, this is not the case. You can always enjoy spending time with your friends and family or engaging in experiences that do not cost money, or that cost very little, and these experiences can still be incredibly fulfilling. Focus on experiencing your loved ones or engaging in fun experiences rather than trying always to make everything extravagant and revolving around money. Going for walks in the park, enjoying backyard barbecues, and even just spending time together over a cup of tea or coffee can all be enjoyable ways to spend time together without having to spend any significant chunk of change to do it. Be creative about how you spend your time together and learn how to invest yourself into the experience so that you are more likely to enjoy having your time together with loved ones, or even by yourself. Learn how to stop worrying about the past or future and instead engage at the moment and enjoy yourself, as this is where true happiness can be cultivated.

As you do go through your month, a great way to focus on what you are spending money on and to avoid spending unnecessary money is to use a money tracking app. Some of the best apps include:

- QuickBooks: Allows you to track your incoming and outgoing expenses for both budgeting purposes and tax purposes
- Penny: Logs into your bank account (with your permission) and analyzes your bank transactions to get a feel for what your spending habits are

like, and then generates a budget for you based off of this information; you can also track your spending habits in the app

- Clarity Money: Like Penny except more in depth, Clarity Money uses machine intelligence to develop a budget for you and give you insight on how you can better reach your money goals
- Wally: Tracks your spending; not necessarily a budgeting tool but will show you where you are spending your money by tracking it all for you
- Mint: Tracks your spending and helps you create and stick to financial goals

All of these apps can help you by giving you space to write down every purchase you make and how much it was valued at so that you are always keeping track of every dollar that you earn. This may seem excessive, but learning how to keep track of the money you earn this intensively can support you in keeping your expenses clear and organized. As you learn to save money and prepare yourself for financial freedom, you will quickly discover that it is easier to do so when you are able to account for all of the money that you earn. Trying to save while also being unclear around where your money is going can result in you spending more than you meant to or botching up your budget, leading to a disappointing setback.

It is likely that even after you become used to saving money, you will want to continue using these tracking apps anyway to support you in continuing to stay on track. At first, it can seem odd to have to account for every dollar you spend, but over time it starts to become second nature, and you begin to see how valuable this practice really is with helping you manage your money. When you become financially free, using apps like this is less about confining or controlling your freedom and more about staying mindful for how you are utilizing your freedom. That way, as you continue to develop your financial freedom, you can feel confident that you are maintaining it in a way that will ensure that you can remain financially free for the long haul.

Saving Your Money

Once you have learned about how you can adjust your lifestyle to support you in being more intentional around how you can stop spending as much, you can begin focusing on how you can start saving more. When it comes to saving in alignment with the FIRE method, there are many strategies that you can use to begin saving money and getting yourself into a state of financial freedom as quickly as possible. Below, we have discussed some of these strategies so that you can begin saving rapidly. There is also information on what goals you should be aiming to reach, how you can save an emergency fund, and how you can leverage living abroad as a way to save even more money.

What FIRE's Retirement Looks Like

Before you can begin to save using the FIRE method, it is a good idea to understand what "retirement" means in this method. Traditionally, retirement means to stop working altogether. People often have images in their minds of retired individuals sitting on their Barcaloungers, sipping cocktails or coffee, and watching the evening news to a plate of supper. These days, retirement means something entirely different. Rather than being a way for people to sit around and enjoy doing nothing for several years, retiring the FIRE way means spending life doing what you love. Often, people who are "retired" the FIRE way are still working, but they are working on their own terms, doing things they love, and enjoying it. These individuals are not obligated to work, though they do because they enjoy the opportunity to share their work with the world and increase their earnings through this practice.

When you aim to retire with FIRE, you are likely not going to be sitting around doing nothing and enjoying the nothingness all of your life. Although there may be some times like this, these times will be intentional. When you are not sitting around, you can do the work you love, explore the world, and begin enjoying your life with the freedom that you have earned by creating your own state of financial freedom. This is essentially the same strategy that most travel bloggers, fashion bloggers, and other people who live abroad or live a modern nomad life use. Through this method, they can make plenty of money and continue living a comfortable and free life without having to worry about their bills and finances or anything else.

Some of the different lifestyles are often given various names within the FIRE community.

- Lean FIRE is for people who plan to live a minimal lifestyle by cutting a lot of expenses and having a very high savings rate.
- FIRE is the middle ground.

- FAT FIRE is for people who plan to live a more lavish lifestyle.

Whatever is your goal depending heavily on your financial options and your values of how to live life. Most people, however, are in the Lean Fire category, about 20% in the FIRE category and only a few in the FAT FIRE category.

Savings Goals, 25X Your Annual Expenses

Before you start saving money, you need to have a goal of how much you want to have saved so that you know what you are working toward. When you are setting your goals you want to consider what your lifestyle is, how much money you spend on average, and how much you desire to be spending on average. Other savings strategies will often advise you to save anything from 3 months' worth of expenses to one years' worth. If you are saving with the FIRE method, you actually want to be saving 25x your annual expenses.

Rich Ramassini, senior vice president and director of sales and strategy performance at PNC investments, states that aiming to save 25X your annual expenses means that you will never be without funds in your lifetime. In his calculations, this is where true financial freedom lies, so it is what everyone should be aiming toward. Getting your savings to account to 25X your annual income may sound intimidating, but you will quickly learn that it is not nearly as challenging as you think it would be.

Below are some examples of different lifestyles and the actual savings amount one would need in order to have saved 25X their annual expenses living these lifestyles. These lifestyles are based on the average median costs of living in the United States.

Lifestyle	Expenses	Rent	Total	25X Savings
Single Person, Per Year	$13,200	$36,000	$49,200	$1.23 Million
University Student, Per Year	$10,224	$36,000	$46,224	$1.16 Million
Four Person Family, Per Year	$48,540	$48,000	$96,540	$2.41 Million

Creating an Emergency Fund

When it comes to saving money, it is always ideal to have an emergency fund as well as a general savings account. Your emergency fund should be money that is easy to access in case of an emergency, and that will provide you with enough money to get by for a set period of time. Often, the initial number of having enough funds for 3-12 months of bills is an ideal number for your emergency fund, although it should not account for your entire savings.

It is important that you keep your emergency fund separate, as some savings bonds can require you to leave your money alone for an extended period of time and can come with hefty penalties if you don't. If you begin to dip into these funds, you will also interrupt your entire savings plan that you have put in place for your long term retirement. Instead of dipping into these funds and paying penalties, it is a better idea to *know* that you are going to have a chance at running into problems and save for it right from the start. Although we all hope that we will never need to tap into an emergency fund, emergencies can happen, and they can leave us with massive troubles if we are not careful.

Although the ranges vary, ideally you should save enough money to keep you afloat for six to twelve months in your emergency fund. This ensures that your fund is large enough to account for larger periods of emergency, just in case something particularly horrible happens. Again, you hope that you will never need to access this money, but having it readily available so that you know that it is there if you need it is important. This will not only keep you financially independent and secure, but it will also give you peace of mind so that you can feel confident that you will always be cared for should anything ever happen to you.

Strive to Save 40-60% of Your Income

Most individuals who are developing financial freedom using the FIRE method will strive to save 40-60% of their total income. Although it may seem challenging to save this much of your income, the more you can save the better your chances are at developing financial independence quickly as you ensure that you have a great deal of money going into your savings account. This is how you can achieve total financial independence and the ability to retire by as young as 30, depending on how old you are when you start. Remember, the goal is not necessarily to retire and do nothing, but instead to retire and do what you love for the remainder of the time.

For those who are truly devoted to saving a large amount of money and retiring young, committing to saving this amount of cash is necessary. This is how you can ensure that you are going to be able to keep aside enough that you have plenty of cash to play with, regardless of what situations may cross your path. If you are not presently in a position where you can save 40-60% of your income, adjusting your lifestyle to create the opportunity for you to have this added cash available is important to ensure that you are working toward creating this increased cash flow for savings in your life. The more you work toward cutting costs and eliminating unnecessary expenses, the easier it will be for you to start saving added money. If you are in a position where you have cut all your costs, and you are still not saving much, you might consider finding a side gig or doing something above and beyond your present line of work to increase the number of funds that you can put into your savings account.

Living Abroad to Save Money

Believe it or not, living abroad is a great opportunity for you to save more money that you could be saving at home—if you do it properly. These days, many people who want to embrace the freedom lifestyle and live like a nomad find themselves living abroad as an opportunity to save money and attain their FIRE freedom faster. Many people believe that living abroad would be too expensive, and while some forms of living abroad might be more expensive, there are plenty of ways that you can do it so that you can enjoy freedom and fun while also developing your financial independence.

The first step in developing freedom and being able to save through living abroad is putting yourself in the position where you can release all of your belongings and actually move abroad. You should also make sure that you have enough money to get through the first few months of living in your new location so that you can reasonably handle any and all expenses that will come with this move. You can discover how much you should have saved by determining what the cost of living will be for your chosen location and saving up enough for 3-6 months' worth of living in that location.

Typically speaking, the cheapest and safest places to live abroad include places like:

- Vilnius, Lithuania: Consistently ranks as fastest Wi-Fi in the world, averages about $425 US per month for rental fees, and has a great night life
- Qingdao, China: Warmer winters and cooler summers, beautiful sandy beaches, inexpensive phone plans, rental fees are approximately $435 US per month
- Cape Town, South Africa: Known for attracting techies and digital nomads due to its views and offerings, approximately $766 US per month in rental fees
- Valencia, Spain: Most cafes offer free Wi-Fi, there is an excellent metro system for inner city

travel, you can live in a sea-view apartment for approximately $1,300 US per month

- Ho Chi Minh City, Vietnam: The energy and culture of this city is often what attracts people to stay, as well it only costs about $440 US per month for rent, and $0.88 per meal.
- Santiago, Chile: Fast and free internet, edgy environment, plenty of activities to engage in, approximately $500 US per month for rental fees
- Ko Samui, Thailand: Beautiful island, easily accessible by flight, plenty of free Wi-Fi, plenty to do, you can pay anywhere from $258 US per month for a room up to $1,000 US per month for an entire villa with a pool
- Tallinn, Estonia: Declared internet access as being a human right, free Wi-Fi is literally everywhere, the landscape is beautiful, it costs about $530 US per month to rent a home
- Chiang Mai, Thailand: Balmy weather, great local culture that engages with visitors, buzzing night life, approximately $375 US per month in rental fees
- Johor Bahru, Malaysia, and Singapore: Live in Johor Bahru, Malaysia and bus to Singapore for plenty of free Wi-Fi, rent an apartment for approximately $336 US per month, enjoy the high quality lifestyle of Singapore with the inexpensive prices of Malaysia

These are all places where you can find high-quality living arrangements for much less than the cost of living in Central America. You can do your research on which areas are going to be the most cost effective to live in for you, as well as which areas you are actually interested in living in. You may also want to make a plan to live in a few areas if you decide that you are not going to stay in any one place for longer than a set period of time.

Once you have chosen your place to stay, you want to make sure that you manage all of your legal obligations. Typically, if you want to live for any period of time in a new country, you will need to obtain a VISA so that you can gain legal entry into these countries. There are two ways that you can do this: the first is that you gain a work opportunity in the new country and apply for a work VISA, assuming that your new employer will be willing to sign it for you. This is a great opportunity to live abroad and make consistent cash while also living for less than the average cost of living in Central America. The other way would be to live as a true nomad and simply get a travel VISA and spend a few months in each location, ensuring that you are leaving well within your legal VISA range.

The latter option is a great choice if you have already developed an opportunity for you to work remotely, such as by working on your computer. This enables you to continue making cash regardless of where you are, while also giving you the opportunity to live abroad and enjoy freedom early on in your path. Many people who choose to live abroad will choose to do both of these so that they can continue to make plenty of cash to save toward their financial freedom.

Another great tool that you should take advantage of when it comes to living as a digital nomad is Facebook, as Facebook groups have plenty of great information to help you achieve this lifestyle. On Facebook, you can tune into digital nomad groups filled with people who have likely already traveled to the places that you desire to travel to, which makes it easier for you to access great advice around how you can do it while still living within your means.

When you choose to travel abroad and use this as a tool to save money, you allow yourself the opportunity to live a fun and often quite a luxurious lifestyle for a fraction of the cost that it would be in America. As a result, you are able to experience financial freedom *plus* a lavish lifestyle in a fraction of the time. If you are looking to get into your freedom based lifestyle as soon as possible and travel interests you, using travel as a tool to support you in saving cash, becoming financially independent, and having an early retirement is a great option.

If You Save This, You'll Have That

The average savings account interest rate is only 0.06%, with some of the lowest rates running as low as 0.01%. These rates are far too small for anyone who is looking to gain financial independence as they will not withstand inflation, meaning that your money will not earn you the financial freedom that you desire. If you want to get yourself set up for financial independence, you need to begin looking into savings accounts that yield higher interest rates. Often, this comes from saving through mutual bonds or other similar savings methods that offer you higher interest. You will learn more about investments in the next chapter, but for now, you should understand that these types of savings strategies are far more effective than a standard savings account. Through investing in the right account, you can save enough for you to achieve and maintain financial independence as your cash will increase alongside the inflation rates.

Below is a graph of common savings interest rates and how much you will earn on top of your money if you invest in savings accounts that have these rates. This graph is based on if you were to invest $100 into a savings account.

Common Savings Rates for Savings Accounts and High-Interest Savings Accounts:

Interest Rate	Amount Invested	After 10 Year of Growth
0.06%	$100.00	$100.60
1.00%	$100.00	$110.00
1.35%	$100.00	$114.35
2.30%	$100.00	$125.53
3.15%	$100.00	$136.36
4.00%	$100.00	$148.00

Common Savings Rates for low cost Mutual Funds and ETFs:

Interest Rate	Amount Invested	After 1 Year of Growth
5%	$100.00	$162.89
8%	$100.00	$215.89
10%	$100.00	$259.37
12%	$100.00	$310.58
15%	$100.00	$404.56

As you can see, investing in mutual funds and ETFs is far more effective than investing in savings accounts. Many people get looped into the idea of believing that a high-interest savings account will be enough to protect them against interest because of the way that these accounts are marketed, but the reality is that they are not. You will need to ensure that you are saving in a higher savings fund so that you can make your money back from your investments. According to one leading financial advisor, you should be seeking to get your funds into accounts that offer 12% minimum when it comes to saving your cash. Anything lower than that and you will not accumulate enough interest over time to really secure your financial independence and hedge you against inflation that will inevitably happen over time.

Chapter 3: Approach Financial Freedom

As you continue to save funds, you are going to want to work toward investing your funds so that you can accumulate even more wealth over time. While savings accounts and mutual funds are a great opportunity to save your cash, using investment strategies will help you grow your cash so that you can continue to increase your net worth over time. There are many ways that you can approach your investment practice to really begin increasing your net worth. In this chapter, you are going to learn about how you can prepare to invest your money and how you can choose what types of investments to get involved in. This is a great way to ensure that your investments are rapidly moving you toward the financial independence that you desire.

Perhaps the biggest reason why investing your money is important is because this is how you are going to be able to retire early. When you invest your funds properly, they continue to grow which essentially means that you can replace your paychecks with your investments over time. As a result, you will find yourself in a position where you are able to enjoy an even more freedom based lifestyle with the opportunity to do anything you desire. Again, most FIRE method individuals will choose to continue building cash through a method like blogging, offering online products or services, or even doing random work in the places that they live. To retire the FIRE way does not mean that you are not going to work ever again, but instead, it takes the pressure off of having to work a job that you hate making barely enough to make ends meet. Most FIRE method individuals believe that work is of high value and that they can and should work on a consistent basis as it is a powerful way to fulfill your inner need to *do* something and be valued for it. However, they position themselves in a way where they do not have to work, so every piece of work they choose to take on is based on what they are passionate about rather than what they have to do. This is where the experience of freedom truly sinks in.

Preparing to Invest Your Money

Believe it or not, there is some preparation work that needs to be done when it comes to investing your money. The first is that you are going to need to know why you want to invest your money in the first place— or what your goals with that money are. The best way to make this plan is to decide how long you need this money to be invested for, so that you know when you are going to need to have your money back by. Since you are looking to retire within the next 5-20 years, you will want to focus on making investments that are going to help you get your money back well within that time frame.

Aside from knowing your timeline for how long you want to be invested in something, you also need to have an idea of how much you want to earn back from each investment. From the last chapter, you already have an idea as to how much you want to have saved, so now you need to determine how each strategic investment is going to serve your overall savings goal. For example, if you have a hefty savings goal, such as $2.25 million savings goal, saving too much in low-yield bonds is only going to result in you slowing down your growth rates. You want to have your money invested in something that is going to pay you back proportionately to ensure that you are effectively working toward your goals.

When you are considering investing, it is also important that you look at the overall requirements of certain investment types as well. Some investment strategies do require you to have a certain amount of funds available, or a certain income per year to ensure that you are investing in a way that will not cause you financial hardships. The information around what these requirements are can easily be located online by doing a search for the investment style you are interested in and your local laws surrounding those investments.

Choosing Your Investments

When it comes to creating your financial freedom, choosing the right investments is necessary to ensure that your finances grow in a way that is effective for your goals. There are many ways that you can invest your money, so it is important to understand what investments are going to benefit you the most and how you can take full advantage of those investments. In this section, we are going to go over which investments are the smartest options for those who want to use FIRE methods to create financial freedom.

The FIRE method typically works best with two types of investments: ETFs and index funds, and the stock market. Investing in ETFs and index funds is excellent because they are low cost investments that will allow you to take charge of your own funds with zero need for support from anyone else. Investing in stock funds is ideal because over time they always rise, so as long as you get invested into the right company and are willing to keep your funds invested for several months, or even years, you can feel confident that you are going to get a strong return on your investment. It is important that you invest learn to invest on your own, as financial advisors are not effective in helping you get the results that you desire. Remember, they have their own incentives and desires for investing, and their intentions to earn cash will always come above your needs with your money. They will most often act in their own best interest before they will act in yours, so avoid investing with financial advisors under most circumstances.

ETFs and Index Funds

ETF and Index Funds tend to be the best investment option for anyone who is seeking to protect themselves against inflation and maintain their financial independence long-term. When it comes to getting involved in ETFs and Index Funds you should be focused on managing your portfolio yourself. Often, allowing someone else to manage your portfolio can leave you exposed to having your funds being mishandled by people who may not be investing with the same goal as you are. Although they can identify your goals and offer you solutions or financial investment strategies, at the end of the day most professional advisors or financial management companies have their own goals that they will prioritize over yours when it comes to handling your money.

The reason why ETFs and index funds are ideal is that they are low cost and simple investments to get into. It does not take much to understand how they work and to begin investing in them on your own, even if you do not have any history with investing funds. As well, they combine time and compound interest to earn you high rates on your investments, making it easier for you to hedge yourself against inflation while also keeping the investment process simple. You can get involved in a variety of different types of ETFs or index funds based on how long you intend to maintain your investments and what it is that you need to gain from them. In fact, investing in multiple different funds is another excellent way to hedge yourself against risks to ensure that you are always receiving growth from all areas of your portfolio. This is also a great opportunity to have different investments invested for different lengths of time so that you can access your money for various goals down the line.

A great platform to get involved with that is well-known in the FIRE community is Vanguard, which is an online investment platform that you can use to get started with ETFs and index funds. Vanguard is a great platform for first time investors or long time investors, so regardless of how much experience you have with investing you can feel confident that you will get what you need with Vanguard.

The easiest types of index funds to get into are ones that track the S&P 500 or the S&P/TSX60. These two are effortless to get into, often have great returns, and are reliable when it comes to staying protected against inflation. The best way to start the buying process is to look at a broker's fund selection and pick ones that have commission-free options. You also want to pay attention to trading costs, as you do not want to begin investing in ETF or index funds that have particularly high funds.

When you do begin investing in these funds, make sure that you choose a brokerage that can accommodate for all of the funds that you desire to invest in. Keeping all of your investments under one roof is the easiest way to ensure that you are going to be able to effortlessly manage everything without having to remember which platforms you are using and where you can access them. Once you have found the brokerage that you want to use, you will need to open a brokerage account that you can start using for trading. Again, pay attention to the requirements to open a brokerage account too as there may be certain annual income requirements in place depending on who you are going through. If you do not yet meet these requirements, you can either select a different broker or put more preparation work into getting yourself ready to invest.

Once you have opened your account, you simply need to choose which funds you want to invest in and what amount you want to invest. Your brokerage platform will then walk you through the process of investing those funds and adding that particular ETF or index fund into your portfolio. Then, all you need to do is watch your account and ensure that it continues growing in your favor. If you ever want to take out some of your funds or reinvest them elsewhere, you can do all of this from your brokerage account as well.

401K, IRA, and Roth IRAs

More great long term investment options include 401K's, IRA, and Roth IRAs, which are all designed to help you save funds for your future retirement. As a part of the FIRE method, these are great low-risk ways to save funds while still having them growing consistently to match inflation. Each of these different funds has its own unique reasons for why they are beneficial, which we will discuss more below. If you are outside of the United States, you will benefit from discovering what accounts are available to you that are similar to 401K's, IRA, and Roth IRAs so that you can take advantage of this investment style.

401K

401K's are beneficial in many ways. One benefit is that they offer significant tax benefits, allowing you to write off any funds that you have invested in them so that you do not have to pay taxes on it. You can contribute up to $19,000 into your 401K as of 2019—unless you are over the age of 50, then you can contribute up to $25,000. Investing in a 401K protects you against inflation as they are index funds, meaning that your investment will increase as time goes on. As a result, these are a great alternative to long term savings accounts. There are certain restrictions that do come with 401K's that you need to be aware of, particularly if you are interested in retiring early using the FIRE method. The major restriction is that you cannot take money out of it before retirement age without getting a penalty for taking that money. This penalty is currently 10%, which can be pretty high considering how much you stand to gain if you leave the money in there. For that reason, you should avoid putting any money into your 401K that you may need at a later date, and instead ensure that everything you put into this account is intended to stay there.

IRA

IRA's and Roth IRA's (shown below) are similar, though IRAs are taxed differently. Traditional IRA's allow individuals to make annual tax-deductible contributions which means that the money you put into your IRA will always be there and you will not have to pay taxes on it each year that you contribute. The maximum annual contribution for an IRA is $5,000 per year, which means that you can grow it steadily. Still, for many people, $5,000 per year may not seem very significant. A great benefit to IRA contributions is that you do not have to be making a certain income per year to be able to invest in your IRA. Anyone can invest regardless of what income bracket they are a part of. Lastly, IRA's can be opened and utilized even if you already have a retirement fund which means that you can have multiple types of retirement funds including your IRA.

Roth IRA

The Roth IRA is essentially the exact same as a traditional IRA, except that the funds within the account have the capacity to grow. This means that your Roth IRA can withstand inflation, making it an excellent option for anyone who wants to save for their older years and protect their purchasing power along the way. Roth IRA's also have one additional restriction, which is that you have to be eligible to invest based on your income level. As of 2017, anyone who makes less than $60,000 per year (or any household that makes less than $60,000 per year) is not eligible to open a Roth IRA.

Health Savings Accounts

Health savings accounts, or HSA's, are a type of tax-deductible savings account available in the United States that allows for individuals to save up for unexpected health-related experiences. These medical savings accounts can be accessed by anyone in the United States who is an active taxpayer. HSA's can be used for any medical expense in the United States, without tax liability or penalty. This means that if you ever do incur health expenses outside of what your insurance would cover, you can access your funds from this account to support you in paying for those expenses. When it comes to investing, this is an important fund to invest in as it will protect you and serve as an emergency fund in many ways.

You can open an HSA by being covered under a qualifying high-deductible health plan on the first day of the month for every month that you are enrolled in this savings plan. It is also important that you have no other health coverage beyond any ones that are offered and approved by the IRS in accordance with this savings plan, and you cannot be claimed as a dependent on someone else's tax files. As long as you meet these requirements, you can open an HSA through your banking institution and continue contributing on an annual basis.

The 529 Plan

If you have children, using the 529 plan is a great opportunity for you to save for your children's future. These tax-advantaged savings plans are sponsored by states and state agencies and support families in setting aside funds for tuition later in life. When it comes to 529 plans, there are two you can choose from: one is a prepaid tuition plan, the other is an education savings plan. Prepaid tuition plans are sponsored by state governments and can be used to purchase units or credits from participating colleges and universities, whereas education savings plans can be used for credits *and* room and board. Ideally, if you want to set your children up for the best possible future, you will want to use the education savings plan, as this is the one that is going to give your child the most flexibility when it comes to using the funds available.

You can acquire a 529 plan either from a broker or as a part of a direct-sold plan. It is important that when you do, you pay attention to any fees or expenses associated with the account, as each method for acquiring your 529 plan will come with their own expenses. This is because they are offered at a state level, and they are underwritten by different institutions, meaning that there may be different fees required for opening and managing your account, depending on who you go with.

Typically speaking, prepaid tuition plans are cheaper to get into as they only charge an application fee and an administrative fee, depending on who you go with. Education savings plans, however, may charge both of those as well as ongoing asset management fees, ongoing program management fees, and other fees. As a result, you may end up paying more, although the cost may be able to be offset based on where you are going to open your account. If you want to save funds, opening a direct-sold educations savings plan can help you invest without having to also pay a brokerage for managing your account. If you do it this way, ideally you should participate in an automatic contribution plan that will take some money out of your account every month on a fixed schedule.

It is important to understand that if you do invest in a 529 plan, your child may not be eligible for financial aid, so you will want to make sure that you have this all sorted prior to them enrolling in an educational program. That being said, the more you can save now, the less debt will be acquired later on. As you know, part of having success with the FIRE method is to have no debt, and passing on the gift of no debt to your children is a powerful way to set them up for financial independence and the option to do what they love from a young age, too.

Investing in Property

A common investment method for people who are looking to use the FIRE method is property, although how you invest in a property needs to be done in an effective way to ensure that your property becomes an asset. Most people think that investing in property to live in is the best idea, though this is not necessarily the case. In fact, these days, most modern real estate investors will invest in a property only to go ahead and rent that property out right away. This way, the property is essentially self-sustaining as the rent will often cover the mortgage. As a result, you have a property that is growing in equity and has the capacity to bring in money for you.

The biggest reason why people invest in property is that it is something that will never completely lose value—as long as you can outwait any drops in the market, your property will always come back to having a high value. Furthermore, people are always looking for places to rent so you can always rely on renting out the property as your opportunity to begin generating a property income. Once the property is paid off, you will continue to receive that rental income, and you can always sell the property if you want to cash in on it. The opportunity to earn income from your investment properties is high, which makes them a great investment if you are in the right place to be investing in real estate.

When it comes to investing in real estate, you should seek to use this as an advanced investment option. Start with ETFs and index funds, amongst other similar savings plans, and then move on to investing in real estate. This way, your money is not all tied up in properties where it might be challenging for you to regain your funds when they are needed. In other words, look at real estate as a long term or indefinite investment so that you do not feel the need to sell quickly. Some people may want to get into the practice of flipping properties, particularly if this is something you are passionate about, but unless you are you should avoid using this as an investment method. Flipping properties can be time-consuming and is not only reliable, so it is important that you avoid this option unless you are prepared to invest the time into making it work.

After you have built a steady portfolio through other methods, you can use real estate investments as an opportunity to get your portfolio even larger and more profitable. The pros here are already listed above: you will gain more monthly income, you increase your equity, and you have access to something that can be sold for significant value in the future. The cons, however, should be considered as well. One of the biggest cons of investing in real estate is how expensive it is, as it requires you to have tens of thousands of dollars available to invest in a down payment for your property. You will also have to pay for upkeep, which may be expensive depending on how you choose to manage your property. Common upkeep fees include general maintenance, property taxes, home owner's insurance, and land manager fees if you choose to hire a rental company to take care of your property for you.

General Investment Tips and Information

It is always a good idea to make sure that your investments are spread out so that you are hedged against potential losses. Furthermore, the more spread out your investments are, the more you can take advantage of various tax breaks and other benefits that come with each type of investment. As a result, you end up actually saving even more money because you are not holding it in a savings account and declaring it as being your present income. Instead, it is being allotted into various accounts where you can write it off.

Ideally, when you create your own portfolio, you want to be very intentional about spreading your investments across a variety of different higher risk and lower risk investment options. Spreading it out ensures that your higher risk investments have the potential to earn you a great profit, while your lower risk investments have the potential to support you in case your higher risks fail. This is the most basic way to understand the importance of spreading out your investments to ensure that you have an active portfolio that is working in your favor.

Most people have different investment strategies depending on their level of comfort around taking risks with their money. Those who are more comfortable may choose to allocate more money toward high risks investments whereas those who are less comfortable may prefer to allocate more money toward more conservative investments. As you get older, typically, your level of higher-risk investments will decrease so that you are able to have more guaranteed income toward your true retirement years. If you are younger, however, you can always choose to invest more in higher-risk investment portfolios and then adjust your portfolio as you grow older to make sure that you are not losing a significant amount of money later in life, should a loss be incurred.

One method that is often recommended when it comes to choosing how much to invest in which area of your portfolio is quite simple. Essentially, you subtract your age from the number 100, and whatever number you have remaining is what percentage of your investable funds that you should be investing in higher-risk funds. For example, if you are 28, you would invest 72% of your investable funds into higher risk investments so that you stand to earn a higher ratio of cash back from these investments. This is a great way to make sure that you are leveraging your investment funds without putting yourself at risk of taking a major loss later in life when making cash back is harder to do.

Lastly, if you do not have any experience with investments and you are still feeling uncomfortable about all of this, you may benefit from finding a nearby individual who understands how to invest. A great platform to get onto to help you with understanding investments is reddit, which is an online forum where peers come together to provide advice to individuals who are interested in virtually any topic there is. On reddit, there is a massive FIRE investment community that you can get involved with that can help you discover how you can use any investment methods that you are interested in trying out. Being able to talk to people who already understand what you are attempting to accomplish is a great opportunity for you to discover exactly what you should be buying into and how. There are also many people on there who can help you understand what the qualifications are for each investment type. Make sure that when you get on reddit and you start educating yourself on investments that you are always double checking and fact checking what people say, because although these are people who can help you, they may not have all of the right information for you. Double checking can ensure that you are not being caught with the wrong information and suffering financial blows, or worse, as a result. As you learn, you will find it easier and easier for you to continue investing on your own, making it effortless for you to start managing all of your own portfolios yourself.

Sample Investment Portfolios

To give you an idea of how you can invest in a healthy manner, I have accumulated some sample investment portfolios for you to take a look at. These investment portfolios display an excellent sense of diversity, which makes it easier for you to gain all of the benefits of your investments. You will notice that we have shared an array of portfolios to give you an idea of different types of investment styles and how you can diversify in a way that suits your needs most.

Aggressive Portfolio

A common aggressive portfolio for people who are looking to save the FIRE method is to use a 70/30 approach up to an 80/20 approach. For example:

Aggressive Portfolio #1:
- 70% invested in VTSAX (Total US equity index)
- 30% invested in VTIAX (Total International equity index)

Aggressive Portfolio #2:
- 50% invested in AAPL
- 30% invested in VBR (Vanguard small-cap value)
- 10% invested in SCHH (US REIT index)
- 10% GILD

Aggressive Portfolio with Real Estate:
- 60% invested in VTSAX (Total US equity index)
- 25% invested in VTIAX (Total International equity index)
- 15% invested in real estate

Balanced Portfolio

A balanced portfolio is often a 50/50 ratio or one that evenly splits between the types of funds being invested in. Below are two examples of balanced portfolios based off of a person who does invest in real estate, and another person who does not.

Balanced Portfolio No Real Estate:
- 50% invested in VTSAX
- 25% invested in Roth IRA
- 25% invested in Vanguard index funds

Balanced Portfolio Real Estate:
- 35% invested in VTSAX
- 35% invested in Roth IRA
- 30% invested in real estate

Conservative Portfolio

Conservative portfolios will often favor investments that are less likely to incur losses, such as bonds. Some conservative investors will include more real estate in their portfolio because in the long run real estate virtually always grows. Very few individuals get into real estate and lose their investment. Below, I have shown you a handful of conservative investments that are inclusive of varying types of real estate investments.

Conservative Portfolio Favoring Real Estate:
- 10% invested in VTSAX
- 50% invested in real estate
- 40% invested in Vanguard ETFs

Conservative Portfolio Favoring Bonds:
- 10% invested in REIT
- 50% invested in Vanguard ETFs
- 40% invested in real estate

Conservative Portfolio with No Stocks:
- 50% invested in Vanguard ETFs
- 50% invested in real estate

Building Your Own Portfolio

When it comes to building your own portfolio, you will want to consider what types of investments you plan on getting into and what types of investments you are presently prepared to get into. Developing a diversified portfolio can take time, as you want to make sure each time you get into a new style of investment that you are taking the time to understand how that investment works and what you need to do in order to manage it. You also want to grow accustomed to allocating the funds toward that investment each month so that as you begin to grow your portfolio, you are not investing more than what is reasonable on a month to month basis.

Ideally, you should start with something simple like ETFs or index funds as these are easy to understand, easy to get into, and typically have very minimal requirements to help you get into the process of investing. They can also be invested into every month, or you can allocate a larger lump sum toward your investment and then leave it be, that is entirely up to you and what is going to suit your needs. You can also look into getting started with growing funds like 401Ks, IRAs and Roth IRAs, as these are ones that you can continually add into on a month to month basis. Although they do require a little more effort to manage and grow, they are still easier to understand which makes it easier for you to gain the benefits of these investments. Lastly, if you want to get into more volatile investment strategies like stocks or real estate, you can consider doing that once the more conservative side of your portfolio has been built out. This way, you can ensure that you are building from a solid foundation that is going to remain intact even if anything goes wrong with your more volatile investments.

It is likely that your portfolio will always be in a state of shifting as certain parts of your portfolio mature and need to be adjusted in order to be reinvested. If you find that your more volatile investments are not working in your favor, you will also need to adjust these to ensure that you are investing in a way that is going to protect your financial wellbeing. Over time, you will want to gradually reduce the amount that you have invested in more volatile investments such as stocks to ensure that you are protecting your assets to the best of your ability.

Chapter 4: Achieve Financial Freedom

Once you have achieved your state of financial freedom, you are going to need to know what to do with it! Learning appropriate methods for maintaining and managing your freedom and learning how to truly enjoy your freedom are both imperative for you to ensure that you are able to enjoy the freedom that you have created for yourself. Oftentimes, once people have created financial freedom for themselves, they may find themselves facing a sense of complacency that results in them no longer working toward creating and maintaining their freedom, or they never fully enjoy it. As a result, the process of building freedom is made less meaningful because they are either sabotaging their freedom by confining themselves again or never becoming truly free from the boundaries they have placed in their minds.

As you begin to develop your own financial freedom, you also need to be learning how to truly free yourself from the beliefs and opinions that you have carried with you for some time. You will want to spend time learning how to truly free yourself so that you can begin experiencing complete freedom from the financial burdens that once caused you to live a very restrictive life. As you incline more to experiencing true freedom, protecting and managing your freedom through the necessary action steps becomes easier because you are able to respect what money has offered you. Many people find that once they reach the final stage of FIRE they experience a high that allows them to realize how far they have come and how free they are, but this high eventually crashes as they realize that their purpose has been fulfilled. It is really common for people who have succeeded with FIRE to crash, potentially even throwing themselves back into financial ruin because of their own inability to deal with this crash. Learning how to find a new purpose in life is imperative to avoid undoing all of the success you have created in your life.

In this chapter, we are going to explore how you can spend money once you have achieved financial freedom, what you can do to continue maintaining your financial freedom, and how you can begin to experience mental freedom. You will discover how easy it is for you to let go now that you have created this solid foundation for yourself and, as a result, you will have the capacity to be made truly free from many conventional burdens of modern living. This is going to support you in fully locking in your path to being financially unchained.

Defining Freedom and Independence

The next thing you need to do when it comes to developing your freedom-based mindset is defining what freedom and independence mean for you. Like happiness, these two definitions are personal and will support you in identifying exactly what type of lifestyle it is that you desire to create. Still, it can be beneficial to know what they mean officially so that you can get a strong guideline for what freedom and independence truly are.

They are as follows:

- Freedom: the power or right to act, speak, or think as one wants without hindrance or restraint
- Independent: free from outside control; not depending on another's authority

The best way to define these two words is to take a journal and write down the lifestyles that you associate with freedom and independence. Get clear on what these lifestyles would look like if you were to be living totally free and totally independent. Allow yourself to really get clear on what these are by dreaming without the restrictions of anything that would interrupt your freedom or independence. In other words, if anything that is presently holding you back did not exist, what would your life look like?

As you define these words for yourself, you start to give your dream or your goal a meaning. Instead of simply having an idea of what it is that you are working toward, you begin to see what it is that you are working toward and you can start determining whether or not your life actually looks like this. Any area of your life that does not yet match these two definitions can be adjusted by using the FIRE method and consistently working toward creating freedom and independence in your mind.

Remember, freedom and independence are not just about money. Someone could hand you a million dollars, and you might still feel like you have a lack of freedom and a lack of independence because you are not yet aware of how to mentally operate from a space of freedom and independence. You need to begin practicing choosing the things that make you feel free and happy and relying on yourself so that you are not relying on other people to fulfill any needs for you. The sooner you can learn how to be truly free and independent in your mind, the easier it will be for you to turn that vision into a reality and start setting yourself up for complete financial freedom. As a result, you will always be able to do whatever it is that you desire, and no one will be able to hold you back or prevent you from getting to where you want to go. Essentially, if it is something that you want, it is something that you are going to get.

Spending Money

Learning how to spend money in an effective way is crucial if you truly want to be able to gain and sustain financial independence and develop the capacity to retire early. There are a few ways that you can continue to spend money through your financial freedom that will ensure that you are both able to live the life that you desire to live and continue maintaining your financial freedom. The key here is to make sure that you are wisely spending so that you can truly stay financially free. In other words, even people who are financially free will still critically consider their purchases and look for deals to ensure that they are getting the most for their money. This way, they can continue to maintain their financial independence while also enjoying the lifestyle that they desire.

The FIRE movement highlights a particular method known as the "4% Method", which is also known as the "Safe Withdrawal Rate" or "SWR", which is used to define how much money you should be spending to ensure that you are not risking your financial freedom. This 4% method essentially means that you withdraw just 4% of your investments when you need funds so that you can continue to allow the rest of your funds to grow and live off of the 4%. So, say you needed $39,000 per year to pay for your annual expenses and live the lifestyle you desire to live. If that were the case, you would need to have about $980,000 in investments so that this money would continue to grow and you would continue to be able to remove your 4% per year for living expenses.

The 4% method is an excellent tool for anyone who desires to live exclusively or close to exclusively off of their investments, as it can allow you to live off of the growth on your investments while still keeping the rest tied up for further growth. That being said, this is not necessarily the most sustainable method for those who are younger, such as in their 30s and 40s. Generally, the 4% rule works excellent for people who are in their 60s and who are only looking at another 30 or so years alive, as this gives them plenty of funds to enjoy for their retirement. For people who are younger, these smaller funds are not going to be enough to live on, especially as time goes on. In order to be able to afford the expenses of life, oftentimes those who are younger will need to adjust their investment ratios so that they are investing in significant proportions if they are going to be living off of their investment gains.

When you do shop, continue to focus on shopping in the same ways that got you to financial freedom in the first place. Keep expenses low when you can, spend money only on that which brings you true happiness and learn how to enjoy your time without having to spend money. The more you focus on creating this type of freedom, the more freedom you are going to have to enjoy. You will quickly discover that spending money without going overboard and sabotaging your freedom is easier than you think. You simply need to remain smart, focused, and committed to maintaining your freedom so that you do not have to rebuild from ground zero once again.

Maintaining Your Freedom

Younger people can choose to live like a digital nomad by allowing for their investments to cover some of their basic expenses while using their passion projects to fund the rest of their living expenses. Some digital nomads do this by offering services or products online, whereas others will even simply create presences and leverage those presences through other brands. A common way that people using the FIRE method achieve their total freedom is through hosting podcasts and otherwise building online presences so that brands want to hire them to advertise for them. That, or they will end up having their podcasts or platforms "sponsored" by brands who want to gain public recognition through that individual. There are many ways that younger individuals can pursue work that they love while also being able to maintain financial independence and retire early using the fire method.

Ideally, you should do some exploration to discover what it is that you love doing and then begin working toward doing the said thing in a way that provides you with money. Most passions have the capacity to earn a healthy income, so allowing yourself the opportunity to explore how your passion may be profitable is a great opportunity to start earning that extra income to help you maintain your freedom.

Fortunately, many young people are looking to discover how they can get into financial freedom, which means that many are learning about how they can profit from their passions. If you want to profit from your passions, you can always look to other people who are profiting from similar passions and follow them as an inspiration or guide to support you in profiting from your own. In many cases, you will be able to find online guides, courses, or programs to support you in finding ways that you can begin profiting from your own passion. These programs will support you in identifying how you can not only understand how to profit from your passion but also how you can build a strategy to do so.

If you do choose to follow a system to profit from your passion, it is a good idea to choose a system that is going to support you with truly generating success. Be careful about who you gain your knowledge from, as there are many people out there attempting to capitalize on young individuals wanting financial freedom which can lead to you potentially learning from people who do not necessarily know what they are doing. Pay attention to who you are following, what they are marketing, and what type of lifestyle they are living. Do not be afraid to do a background check on the individual online to make sure that they truly do offer what they say they offer, and pay attention to their followers and what their reputation seems to be. If you are unsure, follow people for a while and pay attention to how their reputation grows in that time that you follow them. See if you like what they are sharing and if they come across as authentic and genuine. Ensure that you can connect with them in a way that feels right for you. If you have a hard time understanding what they are saying or putting their tips into action in your own life, avoid purchasing anything from that individual as it may be just as challenging for you to learn from them in a paid program. Remember, part of being financially free is knowing how to be cautious about where and how you are spending your money, so do not just spend money in any which way. Spend it in a way that makes sense, and that serves you by ensuring that any program or offering you invest in to support you is actually going to help you grow.

Another way that you can maintain your freedom is through reinvesting your funds as frequently as possible. Any time you have gains that you do not need to support your way of life, reinvest them into something new so that they can continue growing. Do not be afraid to explore various investment strategies and take advantage of what is available to you, the more you do, the easier it will be for you to understand the investments that you are getting involved with. Over time, you will also learn how to manage your money in a way that gives you maximum returns on your investments as you grow to understand which ones are most lucrative.

Using Your Free Time

Although wisely spending your money is important, it is also important that you begin to embrace your financial freedom when you achieve it! Many people put themselves in a position where they feel as though they cannot truly enjoy their financial freedom because they are so terrified of sabotaging it and losing it once again. If you are living in this state of intense fear around money, no amount of financial freedom will offer you the freedom that you desire because you will always be afraid of it disappearing on you. Learning how to free your mind from this fear of never having enough money and allowing yourself to enjoy the freedom that you have created for yourself is necessary for helping you with staying truly free.

Learning how to master your mindset around money and learning how to enjoy your free time takes practice. Below, we will go over several ways that you can enjoy all of your newfound free time and how you can make the most out of life while maintaining your financial freedom. This way, you can truly enjoy all of the freedom that you have created for yourself without the fear of losing your freedom for overspending or making a wrong choice along the way.

Connecting with Others

One great way to spend your time once you have created freedom for yourself using the FIRE method is connecting with others. When people achieve financial freedom, one of the best things that they can do with their spare time is to work toward connecting with the people around them once again. Networking, establishing new friendships, and even just going out and connecting with strangers over new hobbies is a great opportunity for you to begin nurturing your need to socialize. Sometimes, when people establish financial freedom, they can fall into a state of isolation, especially if they are already generally introverted in nature and find that they are not particular toward developing new relationships. While spending time alone is certainly a perk, it is important to understand that obtaining financial freedom means that you no longer need to work, which means that you miss out on the socialization elements of working. If you are not careful, you will struggle with connecting with others over time because you become so used to your isolation and doing everything by yourself or with your partner. Engaging in a healthy social life by connecting with others is a wonderful opportunity for you to connect with those around you and keep a healthy social life after you leave your career and start enjoying your freedom.

When you do connect with people, make sure you do it on a consistent basis. Call your friends and family, go over to their homes or invite them over and enjoy your time together, and begin spending more time together with the people you love. This is a great opportunity to nurture your relationships and start enjoying more stress-free time together. When you do, make sure that you consider your finances but avoid feeling restricted by them. Sometimes, you should go out with your friends and family and enjoyed paid experiences. Other times, be okay with enjoying each other's company at home over a home cooked meal or a great movie. Find creative ways to spend time together so that you can enjoy each other's presence and nurture these relationships even more.

In addition to connecting with other people that you already know, you should also seek to start connecting with other people who are living in accordance with the FIRE method as well. Sometimes, connecting with your loved ones who do not entirely understand what you are doing can be challenging, especially if they feel jealous of your financial situation or they feel as though you owe them something because you experience freedom. Understand that you do not owe anyone anything and that you are entitled to say "no" if people ask things of you. Spending time with other FIRE method users is a great way to stay motivated and connected to people with a similar thought process as you. This is also a great way to connect with other people who understand what it is like to have as much free time as you do, as your family and friends who do not use the FIRE method will likely not have any idea as to what it is like. Sometimes, having friends that are not restricted by their work schedules can be helpful.

Finding New Things to Pursue

When it comes to finding new ways to fill your extra time, it is always a good idea to start looking for new things to pursue. New things are not only going to keep you interested and give you a fresh sense of life, but they are also going to help you really embody the new life that you have built for yourself around freedom and independence. There are many new things that you can pursue once you have all of the extra time on your hands, and what exactly it is that you choose to do is entirely up to you.

Typically, people who attain financial independence and freedom find that they want to try new things because this is a fun way to spend their time. Furthermore, they can begin to do things in all areas of their lives so that they are feeling fulfilled and satisfied in their entire lives. For example, if you wanted to make the most out of your free time, you would want to focus on generating fulfillment with your hobbies, your health, your enjoyment, your family, your relationship with yourself, and any other area of your life that is meaningful to you. The more you invest in making all of the meaningful areas of your life matter, the more you are going to be able to enjoy your life with all of your newfound freedom.

Here are some great ideas of ways that you can spend your free time:

- **Help Others, or Volunteer.** Because you no longer need to work, or at least not so much, you can start using your spare time to volunteer or help those around you. Helping others through volunteer services is an incredibly rewarding and fulfilling way to spend your time, as it gives you the opportunity to meet new people, connect with others in a profound way, and have a positive impact on those around you. Anyone who has engaged in any level of volunteer work will tell you that the work that you do as a volunteer changes you as a person.

It is truly a powerful way to connect with others and be of service to those around you.

- **Engage In New Hobbies.** Find new things for you to do, such as art, dance, poetry, comedy, or anything else that you find interesting. Many FIRE retirees find that hobbies are fulfilling as they help them have something to continue learning about and educating themselves on, which keeps their minds active and happy.

- **Get Fit.** With your free time, you have plenty of opportunities to get fit! You can start going to the gym, set fitness goals for yourself to achieve, or even just get into doing a new sport that you are interested in. Sports are a great way to keep physically active so that you are regularly working through your energy and keeping yourself in motion all day.

- **Spend Time With Loved Ones.** When you work all the time and are often stressed from your job, spending time with friends and loved ones can fall to the back burner. Spending your free time visiting friends and family and building your relationships with your loved ones, or creating new friendships with people who live similarly to you is a great way to enjoy your newfound freedom.

- **Travel.** Traveling is one thing that many people look forward to when they have chosen the FIRE method, as they now have the funds and freedom to be able to travel anywhere they want to. You can work on the go, or you can leave work out of it altogether and simply enjoy living

the nomadic lifestyle with your financial
freedom.

Working on Your Own Terms

Another way that you can give yourself back your sense
of personal freedom is by giving yourself permission to
work on your own terms. Regardless of what way you
cut it, our careers bring us a great sense of pride and
satisfaction, as we love to be able to show off the work
we have accomplished and to feel as though we have
done something productive with our time. That being
said, when you attain financial freedom you can start
working on your own terms and doing only that which
you love and nothing else. Do not be afraid to say no to
work that does not get you excited or leave you feeling
truly interested, as there is no need to spend your time
doing things you do not enjoy. When you are financially
free, you have the right to make the decisions that make
you feel happy and free so that you can enjoy your life
once more.

A great thing about our modern age is that we are living
in a generation where you can still enjoy all of your
freedom while doing the work that you love. Many
FIRE retirees are working as digital nomads doing
everything from writing about their favorite adventures
to helping others create freedom or independence.
There are many different styles of work that you can do
from your computer, so do not be afraid to explore
digital options if you are interested in working for
yourself but do not want to have anything tying you to
any specific location. A simple Google search will give

you plenty of great ideas for what you could consider doing for work if you have not already come up with your own great idea!

If you find that job offers are not coming your way, or that you do not want to be confined or restricted by an actual traditional career, you can always consider starting your own thing. Get involved in doing something that is temporary—like volunteering at local shelters or animal rescues —or do get involved in something that is fully self-built like blogging or selling digital courses. Do the things that light you up and keep you feeling fulfilled and do them on a regular basis. That being said, if you start feeling stressed out or like you are no longer enjoying what you are doing, leverage your financial freedom to help you adjust your course of action so that you can continue enjoying your happiness, freedom, and independence.

Some great examples of people who have launched their own careers with their financial independence include people like Gary Vee, Amanda Frances, Jen Sincero, and Jess Lively. Each of these individuals has created their own sense of financial independence and has gone on to build their own empire with it. Gary Vee is well known for running his social media marketing company through leveraging his understanding of social media and how these platforms can be used to build successful and sustainable brands. Amanda Frances is a multi-million-dollar business coach who supports other freedom-seeking individuals with developing their own businesses so that they can attain financial freedom themselves. Jen Sincero is a personal empowerment coach who educates people on how to believe in themselves and in their ability to make money so that they can live their best lives. Jess Lively is a girl who lives the digital nomad lifestyle and teaches people how to embrace the same lifestyle so that they can enjoy life on the go. Each of these individuals has generated personal financial freedom for themselves, and now, they work out of the passion for what it is that they are doing—as opposed to feeling obligated to work every day of their life.

People who choose to work even though they are financially free are some of the happiest people as they are doing the work that they genuinely love and serving in a way that feels good. The truth is, work is something that people love doing, we love that sense of accomplishment, yet we want to get it in a way that aligns with what we actually like. As you step into financial freedom, you can start doing the work that you love doing and enjoying the freedom that you love enjoying so that it never truly feels like you are working. As the saying goes: "If you do what you love, you will never work a day in your life." Such is true with the type of work that people engage with when they have adapted to the FIRE lifestyle and have achieved true financial freedom.

Success Story: Vicki Robin

Vicki Robin is a 72-year-old woman who essentially pioneered the FIRE method for the millennial age. Robin coauthored a book that became a bestseller in 1992 titled *Your Money or Your Life*. Upon learning about the FIRE movement in her 71st year of life, Robin came to realize that she had a major influence on millennials seeking to obtain financial freedom for themselves through the words that she had written in her book. Robin made it clear that we had to start taking our money seriously if we were ever going to experience true joy and freedom in our lives. As the title suggests, we would be required to understand that our time is the equivalent to the amount of money that we make and if we are not making wise decisions, then we are literally trading our lives away for things that are not truly serving us. For example, if you earn $300 a day and you find a pair of shoes that will cost you $100 to buy, you need to decide if owning a pair of $100 shoes is truly worth a third of your day. If they genuinely bring you happiness and joy, then you may be able to justify them. However, if they will not then spend one-third of your day, earning money to be able to afford them seems ridiculous.

Many people who have read Robin's book claim that the book changed the entire trajectory of their lives. People who were in their early 30s and living on their parent's sofas were now able to enjoy financial independence by following the techniques offered by Robins in her book. People who were previously scraping by or unsure as to how they could possibly adapt to their financial stressors were now finding ways to begin enjoying financial freedom and living the lives that they desired. Although she had no idea, in the early 2000s and 2010s, Robin became quite the popular icon amongst the FIRE method users, many of which swear that her book is what got them started in the first place.

Robin never spent any time on Wall Street, nor did she ever have a major background in finances. Instead,

Robin taught about something that many people forget as being important: common sense. She taught individuals how to understand the value of their time, how to redefine what mattered most to them, and how to start living lives that fit those definitions. As a result, they were able to start enjoying financial freedom because they got their values sorted out and they stayed focus on creating lives that fulfilled their true desires.

Success Story: Jeremy and Winnie

Jeremy and Winnie are a couple who did not believe in the traditional methods of living as proposed by most modern societies. The idea of going to school, getting good grades, and getting good careers to help them buy a house, work for 30+ years paying off that house, and retire on a golf course never fit with their desires. These two realized early on that they did not want to enjoy the traditional idea of retirement and success because to them it seemed very restrictive and uncomfortable. Jeremy and Winnie realized that life had far more to offer than a bleak timeline of events that were already predetermined long before they ever arrived. Instead, they wanted to experience life, travel the world, and enjoy the finer things about living right away and not have to wait for a retirement that may never generate enough money for them to succeed with, anyway.

These two were willing to change the recipe to success, and they did so using the FIRE method so that they could obtain financial independence. They started by living in a small apartment in an old building where they would either walk or bike to all of their destinations to avoid having to own a car and pay for all of the expenses that would come with owning a car. They prepared their own meals in their own kitchen using ingredients that they had saved money on, and they learned skills that supported them in being able to do most things for themselves. As a result, they were able to begin saving a significant amount of money which enabled them to begin developing financial freedom. Jeremy and Winnie invested a significant portion of their saved income as an opportunity to begin increasing their funds, and within a small period of time, they were able to start enjoying financial freedom. They now boast about how they can enjoy 52 weeks of vacation instead of 2 weeks per year.

The couple spends their life traveling the world and teaching other people how to create financial freedom for themselves as well. Winnie is the photographer of the two, and she takes all of the pictures of their adventures. She also enjoys cooking and trying out new recipes that she learned from all of her different travel adventures around the world. Jeremy is the blogger and writer, so everything written on the blog is shared by him. Jeremy is obsessed with learning and loves the idea of being a permanent traveler with no official "home."

Success Story: Joe

Joe was a man who wanted to experience financial freedom for himself and his family, so he began making very intentional financial decisions early on. He retired at 33 years old using the FIRE method, and he now enjoys his life in Raleigh, North Carolina with his friends and family. Joe's wife retired two years after he did, and they both enjoy raising their three children together. Joe now runs a company called "Root of Good" where he claims that money is the root of all good, *not* the root of all evil, and he teaches people how to embrace this by creating their own financial freedom.

Joe educates people on the importance of frugal living and saving every penny you make to the best of your ability to accumulate enough wealth to be able to live a financially free lifestyle. He insists that he is different when it comes to educating his followers on creating wealth because he has truly created wealth, whereas other people have a tendency to offer advice whilst having paid off only portions of their present debt. Joe emphasizes the importance of pouring funds into investments like 401K's and Roth IRA's as these are a great opportunity for people to begin investing and saving their funds in an efficient manner.

Joe's situation is particularly interesting as he and his wife only ever worked 9-to-5 jobs, they never started a career of their own until after they retired and they started their blog Root of Good. Through their two jobs, the two of them went from making well under $100,000 per year to making around $150,000 per year. They managed to save enough to have a million dollars saved in 10 years' time between the two of them, even while sharing two kids together.

Joe is a big believer in truly embracing the freedom lifestyle as he wants his children to experience the joys of life itself. He is one of the best individuals to follow for having a true freedom based mindset as he and his family genuinely engage in living freely. You can often find pictures of him and his children playing in the water of rivers, enjoying walks through parks, and otherwise getting outside and enjoying life. They seem to continue to live a very frugal life to this day, and Joe attributes that to being one of the biggest reasons for why he has been able to generate and maintain financial freedom with his wife.

Success Story: Brandon

Brandon is another individual who has achieved financial freedom using the FIRE method, and his story is one that led to him becoming a well-known blogger under the title Mad Fientist. Brandon offers a significant amount of information on his financial blog and podcast around how individuals can leverage their money to begin saving as much as possible and enjoying financial freedom from a young age. His entire website is based around giving individuals a clean cut strategy for how they can replicate the same financial freedom that he created for himself. This is an excellent opportunity for Brandon to take his passion for finances and his understanding of how to create financial freedom and truly begin sharing with those who are looking to do the same.

Brandon retired at 34 years old. He was a software developer who had been planning on saving for his retirement from a young age and managed to retire by 2016 completely. Brandon claims that early on in his life he did not save for any particular reason, but instead he simply wanted to invest in a portfolio that would bring him great financial success. It was through investing in a portfolio that he learned how to create financial independence, which ultimately is what he wanted all along. Despite not having any clear focus for what he wanted in the long run, he knew that he wanted to be able to have the funds available to pursue whatever it was that he wanted to pursue in his life.

Brandon went on to live a frugal life as he continued saving around 70% of his after-tax income so that he could continue investing and living for as little as possible. When he went to quit his job, his company offered to have him work remotely, which Brandon accepted. This is how Brandon worked from 2014-2016 when he officially retired and began living the life he always dreamt of living. He claims that his biggest reason for wanting financial independence is because it is one of the most powerful positions to live in. According to Brandon, a person with financial independence cannot be easily swayed by the people or circumstances around them, as they can easily adapt to virtually any conditions with the use of their financial leverage.

Conclusion

Congratulations on completing *Financially Unchained!*

I hope this book was able to introduce you to the concept of living a financially free life using FIRE methods as an opportunity to create financial freedom in your own life quickly. Despite how people have made it seem, millennials and all later generations are not actually at as big of a disadvantage as we believe. In fact, we are in a great position to be able to create financial independence while also living abroad, traveling, or simply enjoying our own backyard. There is no reason why a millennial or any younger generation cannot develop their own financial freedom if they follow a method like the FIRE method to get there.

Although ten to fifteen years of saving may seem like a long time, the reality is that this time will pass, anyway, so it may as well pass as you develop freedom for yourself so that you are no longer required to work at a fruitless job your entire life. The idea of working 9-to-5 for years on end is no longer ideal, especially as we learn about how dysfunctional this system truly is. Not only do the people working the longest hours get paid the least, but those who do work this entire time also tend to find themselves incredibly stressed out and uncomfortable. They do not have enough time to spend with their families—they may be upset because they are struggling to make ends meet, and they often find themselves in ill health over time because of all of the stress. Not to mention, people who work these traditional jobs rarely have enough time to truly enjoy life, so they miss out on opportunities like traveling or experiencing their kids growing up because they are strapped to a schedule made by someone else.

Developing your own financial freedom is about more than having money—it is about having opportunities and choices. Financial freedom is about learning how you can begin creating a better life for yourself and for your family if you have one so that you never again have to wonder how you are going to pay your bills or what you are going to do if a hardship crosses your path. If you begin taking action right now, the stresses and concerns that you face today may never need to be a problem for you again because you are already taking action and making changes.

If you begin following this financial freedom blueprint, you can start saving up for your own financial independence quickly. Before you know it, you will be enjoying the harvest that you have created for yourself as you begin to see your debt diminish and your ability to start taking advantage of incredible opportunities increase. Furthermore, you will start experiencing life more! As you learn to save money, you will become inspired to start spending your times in more creative ways, which results in you actually experiencing more of life. People often think that truly experiencing life has to be expensive—but this is not the case. We often forget that even sweet and simple things can be enjoyable experiences of life, such as enjoying tea with your loved ones or heading to a family barbecue. Even enjoying evening walks around the block instead of watching expensive cable TV can be a great money-saving alternative that allows you to experience more of life itself. You will quickly begin to realize that truly experiencing life is actually significantly cheaper than most people believe it to be.

If you are ready to begin your journey to financial freedom, I encourage you to step back to the point in the book where you're currently at—whether that be paying off debt or saving up money—and start there. Create a plan for yourself and begin following that plan—and before you know it, you will be enjoying financial freedom! You can do it!

Table of Contents